GURU NANAK

The Singer Divine

"This fascinating book of versified stories from the life of Guru Baba Nanak carries forward the tradition with eloquence and devotion."

— Saran Singh
Editor-in-Chief, The Sikh Review

"This remarkable book of mystic tales makes you live in the presence of Guru Nanak as you go through the ballads."

— Dr Jagjit Singh,
Former Principal, Gurmat College Patiala,
Former Director, Guru Nanak Foundation, New Delhi,
Chief Editor, Atam Marg, Ratwara Sahib

"While I was reading this book I felt it sank straight into my soul and I could feel my soul dancing with each line."

— Dr Jaswant Singh Neki,
Former Director, PGI, Chandigarh

"This book is a useful contribution for understanding the life and times of Guru Nanak. The poetic rendering of *Sakhis* in English poetry appears as a pioneer work that can be called a prelude to the Guru Nanak Studies."

— Dr. Harbhajan Singh Deol
Former Professor & Head of National Integration Chair

"What a delightful little book full of inspiration and yet it stands out in its simplicity. These are not just stories; they are LESSONS IN LIFE."

— Daya Singh
Australian Sikh Simran Society

"The Singer Divine, a delightful book written in simple English, is a work of love."

— B S Ahuja, Advocate
Supreme Court of India

"The Sakhis narrated in this book have been heard many times, but The Singer Divine gives them a much deeper and broader meaning."

— Dr Jagir Singh
Editor, Amrit Kirtan

GURU NANAK
The Singer Divine

stories in poems

Satjit Wadva

Srishti
PUBLISHERS & DISTRIBUTORS

Srishti Publishers & Distributors
N-16 C. R. Park
New Delhi 110 019
srishtipublishers@gmail.com

First published in hardback by Srishti Publishers & Distributors in 2007
First published in paperback, 2009

ISBN 81-88575-97-6

Typeset in AGaramond 12pt. by Suresh Kumar Sharma at Srishti

Printed and bound in India

ਮਿਲ ਸਖੀਆਂ ਪੁਛਹਿ ਕਹੁ ਕੰਤ ਨਿਸ਼ਾਨੀ ।
ਰਸਿ ਪ੍ਰੇਮ ਭਰੀ ਕਛੁ ਬੋਲਿ ਨ ਜਾਨੀ ।।

My friends asked me to describe my beloved
Drenched in love I couldn't utter a word.

For

Zoheb and Ibadat

Contents

By Way of Introduction

Stories and fables automatically emerge around the divine entities and prophets, which ultimately create a magical spell that bind people to the mystique of their spiritual leaders. These stories, in reality, are the devotional longings of the disciples of prophets and Gurus and serve as the vehicle of expression carrying the spiritual message to the common folk. These biographical sketches fill the hiatus existing between history and legend and eventually become spontaneous homage to the religious leaders. The poetic rendering of such stories in different languages is a formidable task difficult to accomplish. But Satjit Wadva's poetic genius and literary sensitivity made her attain an exceptional success in rendering the stories from Guru Nanak's life into English Poetry.

It seems Satjit Wadva has revealed the hidden poetic impulse in the stories of Guru Nanak's life and grasped the discursiveness of Punjabi prose in its totality and then framed it in poetic stanzas with her creative impulse and imaginative delicacy. It is her whole hearted devotion to Guru Nanak that poetry bursts out of her heart and crosses all obstacles and impediments that confront the translator while translating prose into poetry and that too from one language to another.

The most remarkable characteristic of her translation is that she has kept up the logic and narration of the story as well as the stimulating force of her poetic diction. She has preserved what was true and pure and jettisoned what was superfluous and unwanted. Mehta Kalu's excitement on the birth of his son Nanak has been so marvelously expressed that even a person who does not know Punjab can understand every bit of excitement of the father who was not yet aware of the Guru who was later to illumine the dark corners of the this universe.

"Janam Sakhis" were greatly discussed and debated among scholars but for non-Punjabis, this book is a useful contribution for understanding the life and times of Guru Nanak. The poetic rendering of *Sakhis* in English poetry appears as a pioneer work that can be called a prelude to the Guru Nanak Studies. The author deserves all appreciation for bringing out such a wonderful work that will surely kindle the reader's enthusiasm to know more about Guru Nanak by delving deep into his scriptural poetry.

Dr. Harbhajan Singh Deol
Former Professor & Head of National Integration Chair
Punjabi University, Patiala

Home

A little over five hundred years ago
In the year 1469 to be precise
The world saw the advent of a guru
The very embodiment of divine light

His look spread calm and peace
His touch was magic.
Nanak transformed the hearts of people
Showing them the right path

He took them from ignorance to knowledge
He led them from darkness to light.

No wonder then, wherever he set his foot
Into a place of worship it turned.

This was the time when
The state was ruled by Bahlol Lodhi.
The year by Indian calendar was 1526.
The place a tiny village in Punjab

It was a hamlet called Bhoe-di-Talwandi.
Now it bears his name
Nanakana Sahib it is called
And is now in Pakistan.

It is about 20 miles from Lahore.
Millions go there to feel his presence
Throughout the year
Year after year.

His mother's name was Bibi Tripta
His father, Mehta Kalu was a patwari.
A revenue officer employed
In the service of the Governor

His job was to keep an account
Of the money earned and spent
And of the lands and land revenue
In the estate ruled by the Governor.

While Mehta Kalu served the Governor
His wife performed all the chores at home.
They were blessed with a baby girl
Whom they called Nanaki.

In the Punjabi language
Mother's home is called nanaka.
Since she was born in her nanaka
She got the name, Nanaki.

The little girl, Bibi Nanaki,
As she was affectionately called
She was the darling of her parents
Just as much as all the others.

She was playful and sensible
She was caring and thoughtful
She helped her mother at home
By running errands for her in and out.

In their leisure hours, they'd sit together
Both mother and daughter
More like pupil and teacher
The mother told her tales of great men
And the daughter listened in rapt attention.

Often Nanaki would surprise her mother
With questions much above her age
She loved to hear of saints and sages
Quite unusual for a child her age.

And this charming child
Became all the more mysterious
When she played with another child
Whom she called her brother

Her parents paid no heed to her
The others dismissed it as childish prattle
She wondered why they looked so surprised
Why they couldn't see the obvious.

Other children made fun of her
They said she concocted stories
She dreamt of stars in broad daylight.
Gradually she kept her visions to herself

But off and on, she'd tell her mother
I want a little baby brother
I know he is waiting to come
Why don't you bring him home?

Bibi Tripta often heard her singing:

> Come, my dear brother, come
> Your sister longs for you!
> Come, my veera, come

I am forlorn without you!
Where are you hiding?
When will you come?
When will you come home?

When will others see you?
When will you appear before them?
Come, my brother, come
Nanaki waits for you!

Before Birth

Bibi Tripta came from a humble family
In the village Chahal in Majha region
Having grown in an atmosphere of religion
Bibi Tripta was a devoutly religious person

She was a delicate looking girl
She had a sharp intellect and pleasant demeanor.
She was sent to the village primary school
There she learnt to read the scriptures.

But her education ended before it began.
Because her school had no provision

And it was unthinkable to send girls
Out of the village for education.

Those were the times
When girls were married young
So her parents looked around
To find a suitable match.

They found Mehta Kalyan Das
He was smart and educated
He had a respectable job
He had the status of a revenue officer.

Thus Bibi Tripta left her village of birth
She came to live in Rai-Bhoin-di-Talwandi
She was well trained in domesticity
Soon she excelled in all her new roles.

The sensible girl provided peace at home
And that gave her the time and leisure
To pursue her personal interests
She loved to attend religious discourses.

Often after finishing her household duties
She would go and listen to the saints
She found great pleasure in serving them
She thrived on their profuse blessings.

Once, it is said, when she was returning
From a soulful evening in the company of saints
Suddenly an old man with a flowing white beard
Fell on her feet, and said, 'You are blessed!'

She stood there speechless and paralysed
She was thoroughly embarrassed
How could such a saintly man
Touch the feet of a simple girl like her?

Unable to speak, she bent double to touch his feet
She waited for him to bless her
He said, 'O Gracious Mother!'
'Bless this old man, Mother!'

She was but a young girl
The man was like her grandfather
Yet he called her Mother;
She didn't understand at all

He said, 'I am an old man
I will not be around to seek his blessings
So, bless me on his behalf.
You are blessed, Mother!'

She got up and looked at the old man
He bowed his head and walked away
She kept looking after him
Her gaze followed him all the way.

Was it a vision or an illusion?
Was it a shadow of the coming event?
She dismissed it as an illusion
Maybe it was a figment of her imagination.

One day, Bibi Tripta was lying in bed
It was the summer season
The family was sleeping in the open
Under the starry firmament.

She saw a shooting star
It came closer and closer
Soon she felt engulfed in it
She became a part of the star.

Bathed in brilliant light
She closed her eyes
She saw the same light
Within and without.

In the morning she wondered
How everything looked just the same
While she felt like a totally new being
Nothing around her had changed.

From that day on she guarded her secret
She moved about doing her daily duties
But her heart, her mind and soul
Were fixed on the light within.

Like the kite that flutters in the skies
Is bound to the kite-flier by the string
She moved about doing her daily chores
But she was conscious of just one thing.

The light within her
Was growing day by day
She felt light like a bird
Flying high up in the sky.

Birth

Bibi Nanaki's prayers
Were heard and granted
Her mother gave birth to a baby boy
When she had just turned five.

This ethereal child appeared
Like the sun in the east
The stars lost their glow
The fog dissolved in the bright light.

This was no ordinary light
That illuminated homes and hearths

This was the light that penetrated
The deep recesses of minds and hearts.

Mehta Kalu, however, was an ordinary man
A Kshatriya by caste, a Bedi, a khatri
He wanted to consult the astrologer
To make sure his newborn son
Would follow in his footsteps.

He called the family priest
And asked him to prepare his horoscope
Hardyal was the priest and astrologer
He was no stranger in their home.

He had been visiting the house
On occasions happy and sad.
He had solemnized many a marriage
He had performed the first and last rites.

He was adept in making horoscopes
He had studied the science of stars
He knew how to read meanings in their position
He could predict what the stars foretell.

He made a horoscope of the child,
He pronounced in no ambiguous terms:
He is an exceptional child
He will be a great man!

Mehta Kalu asked excitedly:
'Will he be rich? Will he be famous?'
Hardyal said: 'He will be rich, indeed,
For, he will have a lot to give.'

'Will he earn a lot of wealth?' he asked.
'He will spend a great deal,' the astrologer replied.
'Will he follow my footsteps?'
'He will lead the way,' the priest said.

'Will he be famous?' the father asked.
'He will be known far and wide.'
'Will he be a great scholar?'
'He will be a great singer.'

'Will he be a saint or a householder?'
'Both,' said the astrologer.
'Will he follow the right path?'
'He will show the right path.'

Mehta Kalu lost patience with the priest
'Why are you talking in riddles?' he said.
'Why don't you answer my questions?
'And speak a language I can understand?'

Mehta Kalu was a simple man
He had simple ambitions for his son.
Little did he know that
The astrologer, poor man

Was grappling to hold
The ocean in his hand

He was trying to decipher
What he had never before
Known or imagined.
For never before had he seen
A horoscope so grand.

Far away two wise men
Became aware of this event.
They travelled many a mile
To see for themselves.

A Hindu and a Muslim
Both deeply devout and learned
They knew a saint was born
To strengthen their creed.

It is said, they stood
On either side of Nanak's cot
Offering cups of milk.
To see if he would join their lot.

If he touched the Hindu's cup
He would be a Hindu saint
And if he touched the Muslim's cup
He would be a Muslim prophet.

While the family was bewildered
The saints performed their test
O! Wonder of wonders!
The little infant touched both of them.

The priest found words at last.
He said: He is Nanak Shah Fakir!
He is the Hindus' guru
He is the Muslims' pir!'

As a babe Nanak lay contented
He never cried nor sulked.
His mother and sister doted on him
He was very well looked after.

But, even when he was alone
He had a beatific look on his face
And his countenance shone
With a divine radiance.

Childhood and Schooling

Days passed in sheer bliss
The infant learned to crawl
And soon the little toddler
Delighted his loving sister
He began to play with her.

He would go out to play
With friends in the neighborhood too
But his games were somewhat different
From what the other boys would do.

Boys are boys, you know
They enjoy boisterous activities

They shout, snatch and punch
It's their way of showing their strength.

But Nanak was a peaceful child
He would go out of the way to give;
While others were rash and bashful
He was tender and compassionate.

Every now and then
He would slip away into solitude
And sit in a meditative posture
Passers by said they saw a light
Emanating from the divine child.

Often whenever he saw a group of sadhus
He'd listen to their discourses
He was always keen to serve them
And give away whatever he had.

Be it a shawl or a blanket
Or a bowl or a bucket
He just took things from the house
And offered them to the fakirs.

This earned him his father's wrath.
Mehta Kalu had hoped his son
Would multiply his wealth
But Nanak found immense pleasure
In just giving it away.

One day, Mehta Kalu went to Hardyal
He said: 'What should I do with him?
He's my son; I love him dearly
I can't be harsh with him

But I can't allow him to squander
My hard earned money
I have been toiling all my life
To save some for the rainy day.'

The wise priest told him to send him to school.
He said, 'Let him learn to read and write
And let him learn to add numbers
Let him learn the ways of the world.'

So, Mehta Kalu took him to Gopal the tutor.
Gopal had been teaching students all his life.
He knew how to discipline children
And he taught them the basic skills.

Mehta Kalu told Gopal, the tutor
'Accept my son as your pupil
Teach him to read and write
Teach him to count and add numbers.'

The tutor performed a brief ceremony
He inducted Nanak as his student.
Little did the teacher know
He was in for quite a bit of trouble.

On a wooden board called 'patti'
He began the lesson by invoking the gods
He wrote the symbol Aum
As was the custom and tradition.

The symbol was only a ritual
But the child wanted to dwell on it.
He would not let him proceed
Till he had explained the meaning of it.

He went into deep meditation
He pondered over the meaning
He chanted the sound loud and clear
Till it reverberated in the atmosphere.

The teacher was perplexed
He did not know what to do.
His head told him to teach the child
His heart said: Bow down; bow low.

In all his years of teaching experience
He had never set eyes on such a godly presence
He felt lifted on to a higher plane
His life's toil had not been in vain.

But, he must do his duty
So, he wrote the first letter of the alphabet
That resembles the symbol of Aum
and asked his new pupil to copy it.

When he asked Nanak to show his work.
On the patti he saw the figure of One
Nanak had written 'One'
Before the symbol of Omkar.

'What is this, my child?' he asked.
Nanak raised his finger to say 'one'
'Ek Omkar. There is only one god.'
'And his name is truth.'

Gopal the tutor was so enchanted by his pupil
He refused to delude himself any further
He said, 'Take me as your disciple instead.'
He gave up teaching altogether.

Many tutors came and went
They came to teach him
But went back having learnt
Truths deep and profound.

Pandit Brij Nath was a Sanskrit scholar
He was engaged to teach the holy scriptures
Since the child showed interest
In mystic and spiritual matters.

But before he could write the shlokas
Nanak would not only read them
But explain the meaning too.
And his interpretation was absolutely new.

During the course of his education
He created the Punjabi alphabet
Thirty five letters of the Gurmukhi script
And each letter has a spiritual context.

Finally, Mehta Kalu engaged the Mullah
To teach Nanak the official language
It was the time when the Mughals ruled India
And the court language was Persian.

The Mullah was a scholar of Persian
He began to teach his new pupil.
He wrote the alphabet one by one
And told Nanak to copy and learn.

Nanak read each letter obediently
And burst into poetry
He wrote a verse beginning with each letter
And raised it to the plane of sublimity.

The Mullah fell on his feet
He said he had learnt true knowledge
From his extraordinary student.
He escorted Nanak to his home.

Mehta Kalu was naturally upset.
He thought the tutors were too lenient
Because of respect for his official position.
But he was worried about his son.

He saw him lazing around all day
He would neither work nor play
No tutor had succeeded in teaching him
He wondered what would become of him.

He was losing his patience and his temper
Many a times he spoke to him harshly
But never did he raise his hand on him
He loved him so dearly.

Nanaki was always running to shield him
She knew her brother was no ordinary child
Yet she did not know how to explain it.
How can a candle describe the sun!

Janeo, the Sacred Thread

Now it was time for the khatri child
To be formally initiated into the fold
As is the age old custom in households
And families of upper caste Hindus.

It is a ceremony wherein
The family priest chanting mantras
Invests the adolescent lad with the sacred thread
And dictates how best to follow the moral code

For the family it is a grand occasion
Of great feasting and festivity

For the boy, it marks the end of childhood
And stepping into the domain of responsibility.

Hardyal, the loyal priest of the family arrived
He got the floor scrubbed and cleaned
And purified the entire verandah
With water from the holy Ganges.

On the dais he inscribed AUM with flour
Invoking the divine powers to guide him
Through the religious ceremony
Without delay or hindrance, correctly.

Then Nanak was asked to sit on the dais.
He looked very handsome in his new clothes.
His eyes shone with excitement
He loved to participate in anything religious.

He took his place facing the priest
And waited to be enlightened
With eager eyes and attentive mood.
The priest continued to chant the mantras.

Then he brought the red cotton thread
He raised his hand to put it around Nanak's neck.
He said he should keep it on his body
At all times, waking or asleep

Nanak listened carefully
Questions seething in his mind.
He asked, 'O Pundit,
What happens if it gets wet?'
'You can dry it.'

'What is it made of?' he asked.
'Cotton,' said the priest with equanimity
'Where did you get it from?'
'From the market,' replied the priest.

'Some day it will break; then what happens?'
Nanak asked, not wanting to go wrong.
'Then you can buy a new one,' said the priest.
'You can replace the one worn out.'

Nanak stopped the priest and stood up.
He said he was looking for a thread
That would unite him
With the Lord of the universe.
This thread was of no significance.

What good is the thread, he said
That breaks, burns or gets wet
What good is the thread with a price tag
That can be replaced in the market?

Then he burst into a divine song
And sang in full-throated ease:
'Take the cotton of compassion,
And the thread of contentment,
Twist it with austere discipline,
And strengthen it with truth.

This is the sacred thread of the mind
O Pundit! If you have it, give it.
It will neither break nor soil
It will not burn or get lost.
Blessed is the man who wears it.'

The priest was dumbfounded
He got up and put his head
On Nanak's feet and begged
For a glimpse of such a thread.

All the others looked bewildered.
Guru Nanak continued:
'What good is this thread?
That you can buy in the market
That makes you proud of being superior
Belonging to the upper caste?'

It will break or get burnt
Before the Day of Judgment comes.
Then who will protect you?
So, look for the thread that unites you.

Look for the thread
That is more permanent.'
Look for the thread that will
Stay with you through thick and thin.'

'And what is that thread?' they asked.
'Make the thread with every breath
That is the very essence of life
Imbue Naam into the thread of life.
And stay connected to the source,' he said.

'Life breath comes from the source
It is the link between here and there
Take every breath in full consciousness.
For that is truly the sacred thread.'

As a Herdsman

Though many people were beginning to realize
That Nanak was not an ordinary child
That he had the divine light in him
He had come as the Lord's own messenger.

However, his father, Mehta Kalu
He did not approve of Nanak's ways.
He thought he was going astray
And was wasting away his days.

'He is lazy and very moody
He keeps wasting his time

Neither willing to learn nor toil.
What will become of him?' he wondered.

In the rich fertile land of Punjab
The people are diligent and hardworking
They till the soil and produce rich crops
That involves a lot of sweat and blood.

Mehta Kalu had dreams of making his only son
A wealthy businessman or at least
A senior officer in the royal court.
But his son showed no interest
In earning wealth or social status.

Since Nanak showed no signs
Of following the trodden path
He was considered a good-for-nothing fellow
He could at least mind the cattle.

He was sent as a herdsman
With the cattle to the green pastures
To keep watch over them lest they stray
Into fields and destroy the crops therein.

Thus, Mehta Kalu, told his son
'Take the cows and buffaloes
And go to the grassy pastures
On the outskirts of the village.

Go and graze the cattle
Keep a watchful eye on them
And bring them home
When the day is done.'

Thus the guru who was to shine in the world
Became a herdsman at the age of ten.
He loved the job immensely
As it took him into the lap of nature
It gave him enough time to ponder.

Cows and buffaloes, you see,
Are good people indeed.
They mind their own business
And let you do your own thing.

True to his nature, Nanak would sit
In the lotus posture looking inwards
His eyes closed and mind far away
From the world that surrounded him.

One day, as he was lost in his own thoughts
The cows and buffaloes moved away,
And into the Zamindar's fields they strayed
For they knew not to whom they belonged.

Fields are fields after all
And the greenery attracts the cows.

Poor things, they eat and chew grass
Oblivious of the owners and their impudence.

The Zamindar's men saw the cattle
Grazing merrily in the forbidden territory
They shuddered to think of the poor lad
For allowing such audacity.

Everyone knew the landlord
Ill-tempered, haughty and arrogant
They knew in rage he would thunder
They knew he'd take the boy to task.

They felt sorry for this unique child
He was gaining a reputation for being lazy
Heavens will fall upon him, they thought
They prayed to God to protect him.

The Zamindar did not waste his time
He went to Mehta Kalu and complained
'Your son was sleeping like a log
And your cattle have destroyed my crop.
You better make amends
Or I shall take you to court.'

Mehta Kalu stood with folded hands
Begging for forgiveness, he said,
'Tell me the damage caused;
I will try to pay for it.'

But the landlord was adamant
He went to the Governor to complain.
However, Rai Bular the Governor
Was extremely fond of the lad.

He had a soft corner for Nanak.
He decided to investigate the matter
He told the haughty landlord
'Assess the damage and then come to me.'

Mehta Kalu followed the landlord
Stalking arrogantly in front.
They were going to the fields
To assess the damage caused.

Together they went from field to field.
They looked at each field intently.
But all they saw was a rich ripe crop
Dancing merrily in the wind.

Mehta Kalu asked with great humility,
'Sir, which is the field that has been
Destroyed by my straying cattle
And the negligence of my indolent son?'

The landlord looked closely at every stalk.
He had never before seen so rich a crop.
He wondered what had happened
In the time that he had been gone?

'Your son is a magician of sorts;
I swear I saw my crop destroyed
Just a little while ago
With my own eyes.'

The landlord felt ashamed
He had to cut a sorry figure
In front of the Governor.
Yet he could not explain
What exactly had taken place.

Rai Bular, by now, was convinced
That the Lord Almighty had been kind
To send this divine child to his state
He promised to take care of him

His heart overflowed with gratitude
He thanked the powers that be
For showering such blessings
On a poor creature like he.

The Snake Umbrella

The next day and the days that followed
Nanak continued to take the cattle out
To graze in the green pasture
Just outside the village precincts.

It was now a common scene
Witnessed by the villagers
The young godly lad
And the cattle walking together
In perfect harmony.

When he sang the divine song
They listened with their ears upturned
When he sat in meditation they left him alone
When he spoke to them they responded.

Many days went by in sheer bliss
One day, a passer by on his way to town
Happened to see an unusual sight
That scared the wits out of him.

He saw the cattle grazing at some distance
And the young lad sleeping under a tree.
The sun was shining brightly
And would have fallen on his face
And disturbed his sleep.

But he saw a snake
A long black cobra
He had spread its hood wide
To provide the shade on his face.

For a moment he thought
The life of the boy was in danger
And was about to shout and kill him
Then he realized that the snake
Was not a foe but a friend

The entire experience was overwhelming
He ran to give the news to the Governor
Who came at once and saw for himself
This unique child lying protected
By the snake's fanned out hood.

The Shade of a Tree

One day, when Rai Bular was out
On a hunting expedition in the forest
He happened to pass by the pasture
Where Nanak's cattle were grazing.

He saw the cows and buffaloes
But could not find Nanak anywhere.
Then he got down from his horse
And came looking for him.

Far away he saw another spectacular scene
Nanak was resting under a tree.

The sun had moved to the western horizon
It was the peak of summer
And the rays of the sun were scorching.

Rai Bular could not believe his eyes.
He looked again and again
To ascertain that it was no optical illusion
And what he saw was actually true.

Nanak, it seemed, must have gone to sleep
In the morning when the sun was in the east.
There he lay in the same direction
In the evening when the sun was in the west.

But, lo and behold! What did Rai Bular see?
What was it that was so difficult to believe?
All the trees were throwing their shade in one direction
With the singular exception of just one.

The tree under which Nanak lay
Had refused to move its shade away.

Rai Bular was left looking and wondering
He kissed the earth where Nanak was lying
And his heart welled up in thankfulness
He thanked the Almighty again.

Nanak, to him was a guru, a prophet
He was the incarnation of the Lord himself.
He had come with His message
Of this now he had no doubt left.

He even had a stern dialogue with Mehta Kalu.
He told him to respect his son
For he is no ordinary person
He is an avatar of God.

'You should be grateful that
He was born in your home.
You have been blessed,' he said.
'Don't you realize your good fortune?'

'He will make you immortal.
Generations to come down the centuries
Will remember you because of him.
Can't you see how different he is?'

'But that is what worries me,' said Mehta Kalu
'He is a misfit. He remains aloof.
He looks intoxicated like a mad man
He lazes around without a care.'

'Don't interfere with him,' scolded Rai Bular.
'If you can't appreciate what he is doing
At least stop bothering him.
Just let him be!'

And that is my order.
I don't want to hear any harsh words
Spoken to him in future;
Do you understand?'

As a Farmer

Mehta Kalu was a man of the world
He had worked hard to reach his present status.
He worried about his only son
Who showed no inclination for worldly gains
Be it wealth, property or prestige.

What irked him most was his indolent nature
As a khatri, a karam yogi
It is the duty of a man to work
And earn his livelihood.

Mehta Kalu did not want his son
To drift away like wandering sadhus
Who never do a good day's work
And live on other people's doles.

He had sent him to graze the cattle
A job fit for a good-for-nothing fellow
And Nanak had welcomed this opportunity
To pursue his inner wealth.

Now the father ordered the son
'It's time you do some solid work.
Go to the fields and plough them.
Dig out the weeds and prepare the soil.'

'Plant the seeds and water them.
And when the crop begins to grow
Protect it from intruders
And cut the crop when it is ripe.'

Nanak agreed readily.
And started going to the fields regularly.
But the farming he did was again unusual.
He would sit for hours on end
With his eyes looking inward
And his mind fixed on the Lord.

'What kind of farming is this?' the father asked.
Nanak replied:

'I am digging within me.
My mind is the farmer.
My body is the land.
I have sown the seed of Naam.
By chanting it I irrigate the land.
I weed out the five demons
To help my crop grow well.

The rest I leave to Nature
I have done my job sincerely
The fruit will come with the spring
And give me what is in store for me.'

'But what will sustain you in this world?'

'Contentment,' he said simply.
'Why horde for the future
When it is not even sure.
The only thing that is certain
Is uncertainty itself.'

'I came with nothing
And I am doing just fine
He has given me enough so far
Why should I doubt He won't again?'

Pangs of Separation

It was a dark moonless night
The clouds were heavy with rain.
Suddenly there was thunder and lightning
The whole village was asleep.
Only Nanak was awake.

Nanak's mother peeped in to see
Why the lamp in his room was burning
'Go to sleep now,' she said.
'It is almost dawn.'
    'I have slept too long, Mother.
    It is time to wake up.

My beloved is round the corner
And I don't want to miss
The opportunity to meet him.'

This was a new phase in Nanak's life.
From the lazy boy who slept day and night
He kept awake all through the day and night
As though he was waiting for someone.

He moved about in a delirious state
They said he looked intoxicated
Yes, intoxicated he was
But not with wine or liquor
But on His Name

Tongues began wagging
A virtual whispering campaign began
They talked of Nanak's waywardness.
They said he was going insane.

Some said the devil had got into him
Some said he had lost it
Some said his ways were mysterious
But Nanak said he was just a poor simple man.

Once again, Mehta Kalu consulted the priest
'What shall I do with him?' he asked.
'He appears to be sick,
There is something ailing him.'

'It's best to consult a doctor
And get him treated before it's too late.'
The priest spoke from experience
Mehta Kalu looked for a physician.

The Doctor

Mehta Kalu took him to the doctor
He told him, 'This is my son.
He has just turned fifteen.
At this age other boys are full of energy
But he keeps lying in bed awake.

He sits in solitude for hours
Day after day, month after month.
He neither speaks to anyone
Nor asks for food or drink.

He has lost his appetite
He has lost his sleep
O Doctor, please find out
What is wrong with him?'

The doctor held Nanak's wrist
And felt his pulse.
But Nanak said, 'O Doctor!
What will you find out from my pulse?'

'I will tell you about my ailment
There is pain in my heart.
I have been separated from my beloved.
And I cannot rest till I am one with Him.'

'If you have the potion that will
Make me meet my Maker
Then give it to me, quick.
And I will thank you with all my heart.'

But if you don't have it,' said Nanak
'Then admit honestly that
You are no less sick than me.
And let us together find the remedy.'

'Who is your beloved?' asked the doctor.
'And what is this separation you talk about?'
'My soul has been separated from the source.
Like a drop from the ocean

And I am in great pain
I suffer like a fish out of water.'

These wise words spoken
By a boy just fifteen
Helped the veteran doctor
To see the truth unseen.

The doctors only treat symptoms
For the cause they care not a hoot.
They treat the leaves and branches
And totally forget about the root.

Nanak told him the pain
Was caused by the separation
Of the soul from the source.
Until the union takes place
All else are childish games.

The doctor felt enlightened
He had a glimpse of the truth
Clear as daylight
In a flash of lightning

He came out of the room
Totally transformed
He had a beatific look on his face
He said to Mehta Kalu:

'Sir, it is not your son who is sick
He is, perhaps, the only one who is healthy
He is going to find a divine remedy.
To heal the suffering humanity.

While we only look at diseases
He knows what causes them.
He is going to cure the diseases
Of the body, mind and soul.

Rest assured and be grateful
For being the father of such a son.
When at this tender age he knows so much
Just wait and see what more will come.

The Best Bargain

Mehta Kalu, like all ambitious fathers
Was trying his best to settle his son
In an appropriate profession
Whereby he may earn his daily bread.

Now he thought of making him a trader.
Who buys and sells things at a profit.
Every region has some things in plenty
And they are generally sold at a low rate.

So traders buy some things at cheaper rates
From one place and sell them
Where they are in demand
And fetch a higher price.

Mehta Kalu gave Nanak twenty rupees
It was a big sum in those days.
He told him to make a good bargain
To invest it to make a handsome gain.

He sent his trusted attendant, Bala with him
He said, 'Look after my beloved son.
And let him not wander astray
And make sure he doesn't squander away
The money I have given him.

Teach him the tricks of the trade
Help him make a good bargain
Teach him how to multiply his gains.
Take care of him and have a safe journey.'

Thus both of them set out on a business trip
Nanak and Bala went a-singing all the way.
Having walked many a mile
They stopped in a beautiful garden.

At some distance they saw
A group of naked sadhus

They had ash smeared on their bodies
And they were sitting by a small fire.

Nanak was attracted to the holy men
He asked them what they were doing
They said they were meditating
And contemplating on the name of god.

'But why don't you wear clothes?' he asked.
'We have renounced the world.'
'And why have you renounced the world?'
'So that we may conquer greed,' they explained.

'Does that mean you have given up food also?'
'No, my child, food is the need of the body
We have to eat to keep it alive
But we don't go after it.'

'Have you eaten your meal?' asked Nanak.
'No,' said the Mahant, their leader.
'Why?' asked the concerned young boy.
'We eat whatever the Lord sends us.'

'This is our discipline
We don't go out to beg.
We are happy when He gives
We are content when He doesn't.'

Nanak offered the money to the sadhus.
Bala reminded him of the purpose
For which the money was given to him.
'You have to make a sound investment.'

'What would be a better bargain than this?'
Nanak asked his friend.
'Real profit is in giving and sharing
Not in taking another's share home.'

Nanak insisted that the sadhus be fed.
Since they had no use for money.
Bala bought the ingredients for them.
They cooked their food themselves
And had a hearty meal.

Needless to say, both of them got a proper scolding
From Mehta Kalu when they returned home
Empty handed and yet not sorry.
For having made 'the best bargain.'

Mehta Kalu being a man of the world
Had but a limited vision
He didn't know that the seeds his son sowed
Would reap fruit for generations.

Today, when you see the hungry
Being fed in the free kitchens,
You wonder where it is coming from.
To my mind, it is the consequence
Of those twenty rupees well spent.

You see, it is an indisputable fact
Nothing in this world goes waste
Whether good or bad deeds
They come back to you
In many different ways.
And, it's often rather difficult
To link the cause with the effect.

As a Store Manager

In the days that followed
Rai Bular took matters in his hand.
He took it upon himself
To protect Nanak in every way.

He told Mehta Kalu to stop
Scolding his precious son
And on his own
He devised ways and means
To get him out of town

Bibi Nanaki was of marriageable age
Rai Bular arranged a match for her
He found Jai Ram in Sultanpur
To be the man suitable for her.

In Sultanpur, a few miles from Talwandi
Jai Ram was a respectable employee
In the service of Daulat Khan Lodhi,
The Governor of the state.

Soon after the marriage of Bibi Nanaki
Rai Bular suggested that Mehta Kalu
Should let Nanak live in Sultanpur.
It served a dual purpose:
Both brother and sister were happy
And he would no longer be subjected
To his father's annoyance.

When Nanak reached Sultanpur
Jai Ram introduced him to the Governor
He was instantly impressed by this young man
And made him in charge
Of the government grocery store.

In the grocery store
Nanak sat on the Manager's chair
His job was to check the stock
And supervise the workers.

Soon he was recognized as an honest man
He made sure people got good quality stuff
He was polite and friendly with customers
And firm but understanding with co-workers.

But, prone to his nature
He would often go into a trance
And once it so happened
That while weighing the grain
He got stuck on the number thirteen.

Now, this number thirteen
Is called tera in Punjabi
Tera also means yours.
And to Nanak his beloved.

Nanak counted one to thirteen
Seers of the grain
And after that he stopped
He could count no more than that.

For, you see, the journey
That begins with 'me'
It can only end in 'thee.'
And there is nothing beyond.

And then 'tera, tera,' he said
'All yours! All yours!' he exclaimed

And offered everything to the customer
In whom he saw his beloved

News spread like wild fire
The Governor was quickly informed
They said the store keeper was insane
He had squandered all the stocks away
In a fit of mad frenzy.

The Governor was naturally concerned
He ordered an enquiry
And sent his officers to check the inventory
They conducted a thorough investigation
And found the stocks in surplus.

Day by day
Nanak's mysterious ways
Were becoming the talk of the town.
People wondered who he was
His acts were those of a mad man
But the results proved otherwise.

Engrossed in our petty struggles for survival
We tend to forget the different planes of existence
The laws of nature that apply on one
Are often opposite on another plane.

Take, for example, the act of giving
If you give of material things
That which is given is lost and gone
For ever, never to be regained.

But of things like love
Which are more sublime,
The more you give
The more you get in return.
The more you divide and share
The more they multiply.

Saints and sages are traders of love
They deal in truth, bliss and consciousness.
They give the whole out of the whole
And still the whole remains in all its wholeness.

Family Life

When Nanak came of age
Mehta Kalu wanted to get him married.
He expected strong opposition
From his reclusive son.

But, Nanak agreed to marry
And lead a family life.
He was married to Bibi Sulakhni
And they had two sons
Lakhmi Das and Sri Chand

But just as it is not possible to lock
The sunshine in your courtyard
Or store the ocean in your pitcher.
Holy men come to give themselves
To the whole world
And cannot remain glued to the home.

Guru Nanak had two companions
Bala and Mardana.
Bala was his old devoted friend
And Mardana a Muslim singer.

He played the rabaab, the rebeck
When Guru Nanak sang shabads.
And when the kirtan began
People would flock around them
Such was the attraction of the kirtan.

Whenever an idea struck Guru Nanak
He would tell Mardana to pick up the rabaab
And he would start singing.
And forget about everything else.

This perturbed his wife, Sulakhni
She began to grumble and complain.
She wanted her husband to stay at home
And could not understand
His need to go out and away.

For he did not go on business
Or to trade and make money
He went wherever his heart took him
Only much later people got to know
The purpose of his visits.

His sojourns into alien lands
Are known as 'Udasis' in Punjabi
The word has two meanings
One is to feel sad and detached
And the other is to journey.

So, when the guru
Felt the pangs of separation
From the Lord, he set out on a sojourn
With Bala and Mardana on either side.

His wife would be angry, no doubt,
She was worried and concerned
For his health and well being
But she would be totally in the dark
About his plans and his whereabouts.

But, he was always there for her
In times of real need
He would appear suddenly
Whenever she or Bibi Nanaki
Would call out to him.

The Guru went Missing

Once, when Guru Nanak was in Sultanpur
He and Mardana went to the river for a swim.
Mardana came out after sometime
Then he waited on the banks for him.

He waited for some time
And then got anxious
He looked around for his friend
But he was nowhere to be found.

He called out to him many times
He shouted but got no response.

Then he ran to the village
Shouting and screaming for help.

The villagers came and looked for him
The daring ones dived deep into the river
But there was no trace of him.
Finally, they returned, dejected and depressed.

They feared he must have drowned
Perhaps, he was carried away by the current.
Though it was hard to believe such a thing
Since he was a swimmer par excellence.

Three days passed
And there was no news of him
The family wept bitterly
The village missed him intensely.

They had all had some experience
They had felt the fragrance
Of his presence in some sense
A glimpse, a touch that had left
An indelible memory.

On the third day he appeared
From the heart of the river.
He had a divine look on his face
As though he had just returned from heaven.

The first words he uttered on his return
Are recorded as Japuji Sahib
They are the latest news brought back
From the kingdom of heaven.

The Divine Meeting

What happened in these three days
No one will be able to tell
With any amount of certainty.
But the story goes somewhat like this:

When Nanak disappeared in the river
He stood before the gate of divine abode
He met the beloved he had been pining for.
He felt and experienced God.

The pangs of separation dissolved
Like dew drops in the sunshine

It is wrong to say he met the Lord
He became the Lord himself.

For God is not a person
But an experience
Of sheer refulgent light
The spark of which shines
In everyone alike.

This experience ignited the spark in Nanak
The accumulated dust disappeared
He saw the divine light himself
And also mirrored it for others.

The words he uttered are called Gurbani
They come from the very source of existence
Guru Nanak says he has only articulated them
Just as a messenger delivers the message.

Now, a story of this kind
May not be factual but is true
Because it gives the essential truth
But it is described in symbols.

When words fail to describe matters so sublime
We use images and symbols
And the more profound the subject matter
The greater the need for metaphors.

The message of this story is
That unless you die in one form
You cannot be born in another
You have to lose yourself to attain God.

That is what happened to Nanak
He had gone into the river
A young man pining for his beloved
He came back having met
And become one with the divine.

From Nanak he became Guru Nanak.
The sadness and dejection vanished
His cup was full and overflowing
And he went about distributing it
Giving it and sharing it whole heartedly.

Having stood before the formless energy
He saw the divine wherever he looked.
Ek Omkar, he said, for he saw
The one and only one in one and all.

The Singer

Nanak the seeker
Turned into Guru Nanak the singer
The man in pain and agony
Pining for his beloved
Had arrived and attained
And become one with the beloved.

Nanak attained God by singing to him.
Nanak's path is decorated with songs.
He was neither an ascetic nor a yogi
He only sang and sang
And singing he arrived.

He sang with all his heart and soul
His singing became his meditation
His singing became his yoga
His singing became his tapasya.

Heaven is where the divine song is sung
Nanak sang of the music of His abode
Where every creature big or small
Is singing to the lord of the universe.

Nanak's path is strewn with songs
Whatever he has said is in verse.
All his verses are set to music
His path is full of melody
Filled with the flavour of amrit.

Nanak was intoxicated with the divine
He drank unmindful of how much he drank
Then he sang and sang and sang.
His songs are descriptions of his experience.
They reflect the divine within them.

Mosque and Prayer

Once Guru Nanak was a guest
Of a Muslim Nawab
They had many a discussion
On matters profound and spiritual

In the course of their discussions
Nanak said there is no distinction
Between Hindus and Muslims
All are but human beings.

The Nawab wanted to test him.
He said, 'If you really mean

What you say, then come, let's pray
Together in the mosque today
Since it happens to be a Friday.

Nanak said, 'I will pray with you
Only on one condition;
I will pray with you
Only if you pray with me.'

The Nawab smiled and said,
'That's exactly the reason
Why I am going to the mosque,
As I suggested in the first place.'

The news spread like wild fire
The whole village gathered at the mosque.
The Hindus were terribly upset
They thought he was becoming a Muslim.

In the mosque the prayers began.
The priest, the Nawab and all others
Bent down at the right time in right postures
They performed the prayers in right order.

But, Nanak stood erect
He neither bent nor raised himself
The Nawab looked at him contemptuously
He was seething in rage within.

He was just waiting anxiously
To come to the end of the prayer
And take him to task
For breaking his promise.

He finished his prayer quickly
And turned to Nanak saying,
'You are a cheat and a fraud.
You are neither saint nor seeker!
You promised to pray with me
But you went back on your word.'

Nanak said, 'That is, indeed, true
But I had set one condition
Which you seemed to forget.
I would have prayed if you had too.'

'What are you saying?
Are you mad or blind?
Didn't you see me praying?
I prayed in front of the crowd?'

'You were only making the motions
Your heart was somewhere else
While your body was doing the drill
You were buying horses in Kabul.'

The Nawab was an honest man
He was visibly taken aback
He was shocked to hear the truth
He wondered how Nanak had found out.

He had to admit
That his pet horse had died
And he wanted to go to Kabul
To buy another thoroughbred.

'And the priest who led the prayer
He was busy cutting the crop in his fields.'
The priest too admitted that he was worried
About his harvest ready to be reaped.

Thus, he explained to them
Prayer is meaningless
And of very little significance
If your heart is not in it.

True prayer arises from the heart
And then it hardly matters
Whether the rituals belong
To this religion or that.

Milk or Blood

Once Nanak was a guest of Lalo
Lalo was a poor carpenter
He worked for the haughty Zamindar
Malik Bhago was his name.

Lalo was an honest hard working man.
He earned by the sweat of his brow
He was honoured by the guru's presence
He served him with all his love.

But, he was a poor man
All he could offer was dry bread

Guru Nanak relished the food he served
He declined the invitation of the landlord.

The Zamindar of the village was offended.
He invited Nanak to his mansion
He was performing a religious sacrifice.
But, Nanak chose not to attend it.

The landlord came to him and said,
'How can you refuse to come to my mansion?
I have prepared the best and purest feast
True Brahmins have cooked it.'

'The Brahmins have first purified themselves
They have used the best and purest ingredients.
The food has been cooked with water from the Ganges.
How can you eat the food cooked by a low caste person?'

It was Nanak's style not to get into an argument
But let the actions speak for themselves.
He took the landlord's bread in one hand
And Lalo's dry bread in the other hand.

He squeezed both of them
From Lalo's bread milk poured forth
And blood came out from the bread
That he held in the other hand.

Thus, in practical terms
For everyone to see
Nanak gave his message
Loud and clear.

Purity lies not in the water of the Ganges
Washing and bathing do not make you clean
Impurities of mind are far worse than physical dirt
If there is cruelty and dishonesty at heart
Everything that you do is unclean.

And if you must talk of impurities
Then, mistake not, everything is impure
Remember that the milk you drink today
It was first tasted by the calf before you.

There are living creatures
In every grain of wheat
So, pretend not to be virtuous;
We sin inadvertently even as we breathe.

So, let us try to be honest
In action, speech and thought
Instead of getting into arguments
Of what is clean and what is not.

Wali Qandhari

Close to the picturesque landscape
Of the mountainous region of Rawalpindi
There is an ancient city called Hasan Abdal.
Wali Qandhari was the self-proclaimed
Religious leader of this small region.

He heard of Guru Nanak
And the news of his growing flock
He seethed in rage and jealousy
Waiting for a chance to destroy him.

One day, after a long session of kirtan
Attended by a huge congregation
Mardana went in search of water
To take a dip and quench his thirst.

He reached the natural spring
A natural fountain of cool sweet water
It happened to be just behind the mountain
Where Wali Qandhari had set up his quarters.

He behaved as though the fountain
Was his private possession.
He used its water to establish his power
Over men, women and children.

The local people were at his mercy
For no one could take water from the spring
Without his permission
Which was often not given.

He was waiting for this moment
This was his chance to teach him a lesson
And send a significant message
To Mardana's master.

He refused to allow him
To have a drink
From the natural spring
As though it belonged to him.

When Mardana requested him again
He said, 'Why don't you ask your saint
To provide water to his thirsty man?
Why bother me again and again?'

Mardana reported the matter
To his divine master.
Guru Nanak picked up a stone
And up sprang a fountain.

Mardana drank to his heart's content
The local people were overjoyed
They no longer had to depend
On the whims and fancies of the resident saint.

Wali Qandhari was naturally upset
He lost his temper and in a rage
Hurled a huge rock from above
To crush the guru and his men below.

Guru Nanak raised his hand
To stop the fall of the mountain
And till this day it stands
Where Guru Nanak had intervened.

Till this day the mountain bears
The mark of Guru Nanak's hand
Many scientists have researched
But they cannot fathom the secret.

Many others have tried very hard
To erase it and destroy all evidence
But they too have failed
In their futile attempts and ventures.

Today, the famous gurdwara
Known as Panja Sahib
Meaning Imprint of the Hand
Commemorates the miraculous incident.

In Hardwar

Guru Nanak stopped at Hardwar
A pilgrimage center on the holy Ganges.
There was a large gathering of devotees
Since it was the time of the shraads
When Hindus pay homage to their ancestors.

They were taking ritual baths in the holy river
They were offering water to the sun.
The Guru asked, 'Why are you doing this?
Why throw water up when it comes down again?'

'It is for our ancestors,' they said.
'We are sending water to our ancestors
They will remain thirsty and in pain
If we don't send them the water of the Ganges.'

Guru Nanak saw the sun worshippers
They were offering water to the sun.
They told him to join them in the prayer.
Guru Nanak readily agreed and stood in the river.

He too started throwing water up in the air
But in the opposite direction.
The people thought he was mad
They said, 'Why are you doing this?'

He said, 'My fields are dry and parched
They have not been irrigated for many days
My crop is dying and withering away.
So I am watering fields in my village.'

They said, 'How foolish can you be!
Can you be really so naive to think
That this water will reach your fields
Hundreds of miles away?

Guru Nanak smiled enigmatically;
He said, 'You are wise men indeed
The water can't reach my fields
And they are only a hundred miles away,

The simple gullible men
Saw the truth in an instant
If water could not reach
Another part of this earth,
Then it was foolish to expect

The water of the Ganges
To quench the thirst
Of ancestors long dead
And in another world.

This was Guru Nanak's style
He let actions speak for themselves
For they speak loud and clear
And leave no room for arguments.

In Mecca

Guru Nanak saw the distinctions
Made in the name of religion
Were doing more harm than good.
He set himself a mission
To erase all such differences
Based on caste, creed and religion.

That is why he often repeated
There is no Hindu
There is no Musalman.
All are children
Of the same impartial God.

Religions are, after all, man made
The truth however is divine
Religions come and go in time
The truth is, has been
And will remain the same.

Nature makes no distinctions
It sees no difference of this kind
Don't we see the sun shining brightly
On the Hindu and the Muslim alike?

He undertook a long journey
To Mecca, Medina and Baghdad.
He travelled many a mile
Before he reached the holy shrine.

Ka'aba is the.holy shrine
Muslims pray five times
Everyday of their life
Bowing in front of it.

Guru Nanak was exhausted
After his long journey
He fell asleep immediately
Unmindful that his feet pointed
In the direction of the holy shrine.

This was considered sacrilege
The priest was shocked to see this
He gave him a jolt and shook him awake
And pointed out his grievous mistake.

He scolded him in a rage,
'How dare you! O Kafir!
Turn your feet in the direction
Of the holiest of the holy shrines?

This is the house of God!
This is where God resides
You have committed a grave sin
For which you will be punished.

Guru Nanak apologized profusely
He said, 'I am very sorry indeed,
I beg forgiveness for the wrong I have done
And hurt your sentiments.'

'I was so tired after a long journey.
I just fell asleep at once.
Would you be kind enough
To turn my feet in the direction
Where God is not?'

The story goes somewhat like this:
When the priest held Nanak's feet

And turned him around
The Ka'aba turned with him
Round and round.

Those who were witness to the scene
They couldn't believe their eyes
Never before in all their life
Had they seen a scene like this.

This is a story
It may not be factual
But it is true.
Let's leave it to the fools
To fight and argue
Whether the shrine
Actually moved or not.
But the fact remains
There's not the slightest space
Where God is not.

The devout Muslims were stunned
It took them a long time
The truth to realize
They had never before in their life
Seen a miracle of this kind.

When they were more receptive to listen
Guru Nanak sang the following song:

'Let God's grace be the mosque
Let devotion be the prayer mat
Let the Quran be the good conduct
Let modesty be compassion
Let good manners be the fasting
Let good deeds be your Ka'aba
Let truth be your mentor
Let your heartfelt prayer be your Kalma
Then God will vindicate your honour
And you will be a true Muslim.'

The Money Lender

In his native village Talwandi
There lived a greedy money lender
He gave loans to poor farmers
And charged an exorbitant rate of interest.

The poor farmers worked hard all their life
But merely managed to pay the interest.
The principal amount stayed intact
The interest often mounted up
And manifold increased the debt.

His name was Duni Chand, a wealthy khatri
He was rich and prosperous
He had plenty to spare
But he was too stingy to spend
Leave alone to give or share.

Guru Nanak tried to teach him
The virtues of giving and sharing
He told him the joy of compassion
But the money lender was stubborn

Then one day, Guru Nanak
Went to his house and said.
'I want you to do me a favour.
Will you do it for me?'

'Sure, Master,' said the greedy man
He knew Guru Nanak's generous nature
And hoped to gain something from him
By doing him a good turn

'Keep this needle for me in safe custody,'
Guru Nanak told him.
'I am going out on a long journey
And I will take it from you
When I need it in the next life.'

Duni Chand thought only of taking;
He took the needle readily.
But when he realized the responsibility
He knew he couldn't fulfill it.

He racked his head to find a solution
He thought of asking Guru Nanak.
He asked, 'Master, how can I take it
To the next life?'

'Just as you will take all your wealth,'
Guru Nanak said with a straight face.
'But, is it possible to take it?' he asked hopefully.

'You must know the way; otherwise
'Why would you accumulate it?'

Duni Chand saw what Guru Nanak meant.
He realized his foolishness
If even a tiny needle cannot go with him
What good were all the millions he had piled?

'But there is something that does go with you
And it is the account of your good deeds
You can reap the fruit in the other world
Of the seeds you plant in this life.'

'It is the duty of a man of the world
To work honestly and sincerely
And give something to the poor and needy.
While it allays the poor man's suffering
It gives you peace of mind and tranquility.

As a Trader

Once Mardana said to Guru Nanak,
'You make complex matters so simple
You say that everyone can attain God
If this is true and things are really that easy
Then why do we suffer in ignorance?'

Guru Nanak told him that people
Generally get what they desire
'But who would not want to attain God?
Everyone prays for enlightenment.'

Those are empty words
Repeated because they sound well
No one is really bothered about God
As long as he has a good time.

People think of God in bad times
They go to temples, churches and mosques
To beg for something or the other
Once they get it they forget the giver.

It is only the thirsty person
Who knows the value of water
Without the thirst even nectar is worthless.
And the thirst for God doesn't exist at all.

When Mardana was not convinced
Guru Nanak gave him a colourful stone
It was actually a precious gem
He told him to take it to the market
And get it evaluated.

Mardana took the gem to the green grocer
He was ready to exchange it for a carrot.
Then he asked the cloth merchant
He said he would take it for a yard of silk.

Mardana went from shop to shop
Each one saw the stone

And each one put up a price
In terms of his own merchandise.

Finally, he landed in the jeweller's shop
The man who dealt in pearls and diamonds
He had a discerning eye that could tell
The genuine from the fake at once.

When he saw the sparkling stone
He fell on his knees and kissed
The place where it was kept
He thanked Mardana for giving him
Just the glimpse of it.

He said, 'I am but a poor man
I can't afford to buy this precious gem
I would give all that I possess
For just a glimpse of it

You have given me that glimpse;
Now, I want nothing else.
I have no other ambition;
I can die a contented man.'

Mardana returned and related
His experience unique and strange
Guru Nanak said, 'Now you see,
God is not everyone's priority.

It's the connoisseur who knows
The true value of a precious stone.
Similarly God is not hard to find
If on that you set your mind.'

You took a simple stone
And even that was misunderstood
How do you expect them to know
The significance of God?

People think of God
From the prism of their desires
They have reduced divinity
To a wish-fulfilling tree.

'Give me this, give me that!
This is the prayer on many lips
As if God is an errand boy
Employed in their service!

If pleasure comes their way
They feel proud of their victory
But when pain happens to come
There is always God to blame it on.

The true seekers find Him
In the deep recesses of their heart.
Now, you tell me, Mardana
Isn't it really as simple as that?'

At Jagannath Puri

Puri is a town near Bhubeneshwar
It has the famous Jagannath Temple
It is a major pilgrimage centre
For everyone, especially the Hindus.

Jagannath, the Lord of the Universe
Is also an incarnation of Vishnu
The temple is one of the 'char dhams'
Where every Hindu goes to pray
At least once in a lifetime.

Guru Nanak went to Puri
And participated in the evening prayer
Known as Aarati, it is the ritual
Performed by the priest before the deity.

In a silver platter he places
Pearls and gems and burns incense
Flowers and petals give out fragrance

He lights lamps and moves the platter
In a circular movement as an offering.
When the ceremony is complete
Prasad is distributed among the devotees

Guru Nanak was standing there
In the temple when the priest
Was moving the platter
In front of the idol of Jagannath.

Suddenly he went into a trance
He saw the real Lord of the Universe
Then he burst into a divine song
It is known as Aarati.

He sang:

> 'The sky is the platter
> The suns, moons and stars are the gems
> The forests and foliage are the petals
> The winds are the fans

What Aarati is possible for thee?

O Lord of the Universe!

For you, the unheard melodies
Provide the celestial music

O Lord of the Universe!

You have innumerable eyes
But not a single eye
You have innumerable forms
But not a single form

You have innumerable feet
But not a single foot
All the fragrances are yours
But not a single perfume

It is your light that shines through
Creatures big and small
It is your life breath
That breathes life into all

The Guru alone has the power to reveal
True Aarati is the one that pleases thee.'

Sajjan the Robber

Once Guru Nanak along with his companions
Bala and Mardana stayed in the mansion
Of Sheikh Sajjan who was a robber
Pretending to be a religious man.

He had built a temple and a mosque
On either side of his mansion
He attracted Hindus and Muslims
To come and stay in his inn.

He would impress them with his religiosity
He would feed them well
And make them comfortable
But when they began to trust him
He would rob them and kill them.

When he saw Guru Nanak and his companions
He was overjoyed to see such lovely people
He served them well and waited for the night
Then he went to Guru Nanak's room stealthily.

The lights were off and it was quiet
He thought it was the right moment to strike
But as he went closer he saw
Guru Nanak engulfed in a soft light.

He tried to ignore it
And push the thought aside
But then he heard the sound of Omkar
Resounding in the room.

For the first time in his life
This cruel man was terrified
He, who had terrified people
All his life was now petrified.

He was shaking in mortal fear
All his evil deeds flashed before him

He got a sense of what the fear
Of devils and demons may be.

He fell down on Guru Nanak's feet
He wept and begged forgiveness.
Guru Nanak, the merciful, blessed him
He told him to make amends.

The robber turned into a donor
He gave away all his wealth
And the rest of his life he spent
In the service of the poor.

Great saints are so very pure
Like mirrors they show to you
Your real face and form
And the delusions that go along.

And once you know
Whatever is that's wrong
It's not at all difficult
To change and reform.

Encounter with a Holy Man

By now the sight of Guru Nanak
And his loyal companions
One Hindu and the other Muslim
Had become a familiar sight

People saw them going merrily
Singing divine songs
And as though mesmerized
They followed them despite all odds.

Whichever place they stopped
It turned into a holy spot

Where divine kirtan flowed
Like a cascading fountain.

Many were his followers now
They could not miss the kirtan
Many others were jealous of him
They did not want him in their midst.

Once, the three of them
Camped by the side of a well
Outside a small village
Inhabited by Sufi saints.

These ascetics had worked hard
To achieve their present state
They had arrived at certain truths
They wanted to spread them far and wide.

But common people were so busy
In their struggle for daily bread
No one had the time to listen to them.
There were more masters than disciples
At least that is what they thought.

They heard of Guru Nanak's camp
'Oh, no! Not another one!' they said.
'We are already too many
'We simply can't afford one more.'

The leader of the group of Sufis
Sent a cup of milk filled to the brim.
He sent no verbal message with it
To see if Guru Nanak
Would be able to comprehend.

He told the other fakirs
That if Guru Nanak is wise
He will understand the meaning
Of the symbol he had sent.

Guru Nanak received the cup gratefully
He plucked a flower from a bush nearby
And placed it on the cup gently
Then he sent it back again
Without a single word.

Bala and Mardana were perplexed
They asked him what he meant.
Guru Nanak explained:
The Sufi's message said:
'There is no room for you.'

'The cup is already full.
Meaning that the village
Already has too many sages;
There is no room for more.'

'I sent him a flower
That will float on the milk
To tell him that I need no space
Because I am like a flower
That has no weight.'

Guru Nanak was a wanderer
He had no intentions to stay
All he wanted was to convey
That the ego is a dead weight.

And a man without ego is light
He can live anywhere without a fight
But as long as there is ego
There is gross ignorance
That often leads to violence.

The Tale of the Bitter Nut

Once Guru Nanak and Mardana
Had been walking for days on end
Through the sandy deserts
Where not a tree or plant was seen.

While the guru had conquered
Hunger, thirst and fatigue
Mardana could take it no more
He was so tired and hungry.

Guru Nanak understood his plight
He said, 'Let's rest here a while

They found a Reetha tree growing
Alone in the scorching heat.

Reetha is a bitter nut, you see
That has a cleansing quality
The women in good old times
Used to wash clothes with it.

Even now sometimes you see
Your mother boils these nuts in water
For it is the most natural form of shampoo
It protects the hair and makes it grow too.

But no one has ever thought of eating
These soap nuts to quench their appetite
For, they are very bitter, indeed.
And leave a bitter taste in the mouth.

Guru Nanak sat under the shade of the tree
And Mardana said he would go
And look for something to eat.
'Pluck some of these,' his master said.

Mardana had, by now, realized
That the guru means what he says
Even though it is quite hard
To understand the meaning of it
In the beginning.

He did as he was told
He plucked a handful of the soap nuts
And placed them before the master
Waiting to see how it unfolds.

Guru Nanak picked each nut
One at a time and gave it to him
Mardana relished the sweet taste
It was better than any other fruit he'd eaten.

Now you may wonder if this is true
We don't expect nature to change its course
But if you would stop and think
You'd know nature's benevolence

And the power of love is supreme
That overrules all petty differences
It raises the mundane to the sublime.
That is why it is said:

'Things base and guile
Love makes them sublime
That is why the Cupid
Is painted blind.'

Today, a gurdwara stands at this spot
And the tree is still bearing fruit
Pilgrims go there and bring a nut
Some find it sweet and some do not.

Kurukshetra

Kurukshetra is another
Holy spot of the Hindus
Where the Kumbha Mela is held
After every twelve years.

Kumbha is an earthen pitcher.
Legend says that long ago
When the oceans were churned
The pot of nectar was found.

In the tug of war that followed
Between the demons and the gods

Some drops of the elixir of life
Had fallen on this spot

Pilgrims from far and wide
Come here to take a dip
There were thousands that thronged
On that day of the solar eclipse.

Guru Nanak saw men and women
Weighed down by superstitions of all kind
He had a unique way of helping them
To get rid of superstitions and ignorance.

Just as in Hardwar he stood in the Ganges
And threw water in the opposite direction
He had a way of giving a shock to people
To help them see their hollow tradition.

In Kurukshetra he saw people terrified
On the day of the solar eclipse
They would not light a fire or cook food
Because of its adverse consequence.

Guru Nanak told Mardana to make a hearth
He asked him to buy ingredients
And they cooked a meal
And sat down to enjoy it.

People saw the smoke and fire
They informed the learned pundits
The pundits were furious
Because they had been fleecing
The people in the name of the eclipse.

They came with sticks and stones
They hurled stones at them
They threatened Guru Nanak
That he will rot in hell.

Guru Nanak finished his meal
He told Mardana to pick up the rabaab
Then he sang a divine song
In his melodious voice.

> 'In the world whatever is natural
> Is true because it is created
> By the Creator who is true
> Only man-made distinctions are false.
>
> The suns and stars are true
> The myriad worlds are true
> The winds waters and seasons are true
> And true are their movements.
>
> This world is His manifestation
> It is the abode of the Lord
> He resides in it and illuminates it
> O man! Look at the Creator in everything.'

In the Prison

Holy men of all shades and hues
Prophets, saviours and gurus
Have one thing in common
They are grossly misunderstood.

They are like giants among pygmies
Perhaps because they come
Much before their times
And the majority of their contemporaries
Consider them insane.

Jesus was crucified
He was nailed to the Cross
Mansoor was stoned to death
Others met a similar fate.

They went against accepted norms
They broke worthless traditions
They exposed hollow superstitions
No wonder they earned the wrath of millions.

Guru Nanak raised his voice
Against the tyranny of the rulers
He did nothing more than sing verses
But his unpardonable fault was
That people listened to him.

So, Guru Nanak and his companions
Bala and Mardana were taken prisoners.
They were given grain to grind
As a rigorous punishment.

Guru Nanak, the man of God
He accepted the order of the king
And went to the prison
He began to do the task assigned to him.

But, after some time
The message surfaced in his mind.
He began to sing the holy gurbani
He lost count of task and time.

The jailor was obviously annoyed
He said, 'You don't do any work
And what is even worse
You don't let other prisoners work.'

The matter was blown out of proportion.
The senior officials were summoned
They came to take the culprit to task
And teach him a lesson or two.

They came seething in anger
But were turned into pictures of peace
When they saw the grind
That was moving on its own.

There was Guru Nanak sitting
With his eyes closed and singing
And the wheat was being ground
By the stone moved by some invisible hand.

They thought it was a miracle
They reported it to the king
Emperor Babar came to the prison
To see what was happening.

He had long discussions with Guru Nanak
In the end he asked what he could do for him
Guru Nanak asked him to free
All the prisoners wrongly taken in.

Babar granted the wish immediately
Thus all the prisoners were freed.
The heart of the tyrant ruler was transformed
This is the significance of this legend.

As for the grind moving on its own
It is important to remember that
Things happen naturally
Just as the spring comes
And the grass grows by itself.

We are prone to becoming egoistic
We take credit unnecessarily.
But if we are honest, we know deep down
It is the divine will that does it all.

But it is not for us to dictate that will
We have but a limited vision.
For how much of the vast sky
Can you see from your tiny casement?

Similarly nature's scheme of things
Is vast, infinite and immeasurable
Wisdom lies in the unconditional acceptance
Of things as they happen.

Joys and sorrows are but passing clouds.
And in this transient world
Know one thing for certain
There is nothing that is permanent.

The Monster Kauda

During his southern sojourn
Guru Nanak wandered into a jungle
Inhabited by a savage tribe.
They fed on human flesh.

No one dared to go that way
Because many a men, women
And children had fallen prey
They had been devoured by the cannibals.

Guru Nanak went to meet their chief
Kauda was his name.

He boasted of his victories
And wore a necklace of skulls
To show off his trophies.

Many people told Guru Nanak
Of the horrifying exploits of this man
But Guru Nanak had no fear.
He knew the man was not bad but ignorant

Kauda saw three men coming
They were walking in his direction.
Kauda's mouth watered at the prospect
Of a meal sumptuous and delicious.

He lit a fire and put a cauldron on it
He prepared to cook the human flesh in it.
He grabbed Guru Nanak by the sleeve
'Sat Kartar!' Guru Nanak said, calmly.

But to his great surprise
The fire turned cool.
He saw Guru Nanak walk out of it
With a peaceful smile on his face.

Kauda was shaken to the roots
He fell on Guru Nanak's feet
He begged him for forgiveness
And Guru Nanak blessed him.

He said, 'If your cloth gets stained by blood
It gets dirty and you can wash it clean.
But if you suck the blood of others
No amount of water or soap
Can wash the stains of it.
So, avoid such bloody deeds.

Kauda took a vow
To follow the Guru's advice
He gave up his barbaric ways
And spent the rest of his life
In service and prayers.

Meeting with the Siddhas

Siddhas are the saints who have attained
Through their learning and determination
And lifelong austerities and prayers
They bring their bodies and minds under control.

When they heard of a holy man
They were indignant
They thought he had come
To challenge their wisdom.

'Who is he?' they exclaimed
'A mere youth challenging their acclaim

He wanders around in gay abandon
He has not been seen in any mosque or temple.'

'He does not fit into any mould
He does not follow any religion
Then who is he to proclaim
And lead the crowds away.'

After much deliberation
They decided to put him through a test
To see what is his worth
And show him a glimpse
Of their own wisdom.

They called Guru Nanak to discuss
Matters of religion and spiritualism.
The question-answer session that followed
Is recorded as Siddha Goshti in the Granth.

'Who are you?' they asked
'Where do you come from?'
'Does the air come from somewhere?'
'Or go anywhere?' he asked in return.

'Who is your guru?' they asked
'What is the disciple's name?'
Air is the teacher,' he said
'And consciousness the disciple.'

'Have you read the scriptures?' they asked
'Have you done the yoga?'
'Yoga lies not in outward activities,
Look within and find the rest.'

'These are vague replies,' they said
'How can air be the guru? Explain.'
'Shabad guru surat dhun chela'
He said and went on to explain:
    'The all-pervading sound is the guru,
    Listening to that sound you attain
    But to be able to listen to that sound
    You have to silence the noises in the minc

    Listen to the sound of Omkar
    Listen till you can hear nothing else
    For prayers are not said
    Prayers can only be heard.'

The Siddhas were speechless
They did not know what to do
What he said was not in the scriptures
But their hearts told them it's true.

Holy Congregation

Guru Nanak the singer sang
He sang day and night
He sang in all seasons
He sang on all occasions

He sang and Mardana played the rabaab
He sang and people flocked around
Men, women, children, animals and birds
Listened to him spellbound

He sang of matters down-to-earth
And he sang of profound truths

He explained the mysterious and the sublime
Giving symbols familiar and known

Singing, he led them through
The various phases of life
Singing, he revealed to them
The mysteries of life and death.

Singing has a magic of its own
Singing sharpens the higher senses
Singing silences the chattering in the mind
For you cannot sing and talk at the same time.

Guru Nanak's home is where
There is only the sound of kirtan
Kirtan is the melodious rendering
Of all the songs that Guru Nanak sang.

Guru Nanak's path is strewn with song
The divine abode, he says, is where
Myriads of instruments are playing
Where the air, water and fire are singing
Where the kings and judges are singing
Where the gods and goddesses are singing
Where the suns and stars are singing

Where the forests and mountains are singing
Where the birds and insects are singing
Nanak says he cannot name all the singers
To him the song and the singer are one
And singing is the way to dissolve in him.

The Path

Guru Nanak travelled all over the country
He raised his voice against the social evils
He held a mirror to the society
To help them see and rectify.

He saw the pathetic state of women and said
'Your existence depends on women
You are conceived and born of woman
Why then condemn woman who is your mother?'

Guru Nanak's philosophy is simple
'Take care of small things and
The great ones will follow suit
Think only of reforming yourself
The others will learn from your example.'

'After all, only a lit lamp can light another
An unlit lamp can spend a lifetime making efforts
But will ultimately fail to achieve anything.
You can give only that which you possess.'

'Humility is the essence of all virtues
But, beware! The culprit bends double
That is not humility. Nor is that virtue
Which is only lip service and not genuine.'

He explained the true meaning of things
Renunciation is not running away
From home and responsibilities
But living without avarice and attachment.

Live like a lotus in a pond untouched
Like the lotus remains unattached
And like the lotus transforms
The filth into fragrance.

Ego is the root of all ills
Ego is the mote in the eye
It blurs your vision
It makes your life a virtual hell.

Contentment and compassion are virtues great
But man has turned them upside down
If he loses something he feels sorry for himself
But when the same happens to others
He preaches them to be content.

This kind of attitude is not right
And it needs to be turned around
Be compassionate to others
And be content with what you have.

Do not look for faults in others
Because when it comes to counting faults
May be you will score the highest points.

So when you see something wrong
Immediately look within.
And you will see at once
From where it is stemming.

Keep a constant vigil on the mind
It plays the maximum tricks on you
For, not all the people put together
Can deceive you more than it can do.

Mind is like a monkey
That is constantly restless
Even if you slightly loosen the grip
It will take you right into the ditch.

So, the trick is to remain in control
Tighten your grip on the fickle mind
Watch it closely and continuously
And look through the games it plays.

The Last Phase

In those times of primitive means
Guru Nanak undertook five long journeys
To the east, west, north and south of the country
And even far beyond its boundaries.

Bala the Hindu, and Mardana the Muslim
Went with him demonstrating his assertion
That there are no Hindus or Muslims
The distinctions are false and must be shunned.

Finally, after twenty five years of travel
He settled down in Kartarpur

He tilled the land and became a farmer
Till the last day of his life.

One day, as he was working in the field
A young man came to him and said,
'I am Lehna.' Lehna in Punjabi means
A creditor who comes to collect his dues.

'So, you have come at last,'
Guru Nanak said.
'I have been waiting for you.
'I have to pay your debt.'

As one lamp lights another
Guru Nanak passed on his spirit
To Lehna whom he called Angad
'You are a part of me,' he said.

And when the time came for departure
Once again there was much commotion
The Hindus wanted to cremate his body
The Muslims wanted to bury it.

The pundits and mullahs
Made the necessary preparations
But when they lifted the sheet
They found a bunch of flowers.

Thus, even after his departure
He left a significant lesson
For all of them to ponder over
You see, flowers have no religion.

Let's for a moment pause
And think of flowers
It is their nature
To bloom and blossom
To sing and dance
To spread fragrance
To present a happy face
And spread happiness around.

They grow in filth and stink
And change it into fragrance
They know not of any distinctions
They only give unconditionally

They leave a soft perfume
Even in the hand
That crushes them.
Beautiful they are
They beautify the world.

This world is the divine garden
Full of flowers of all hues
They enjoy nature's bounties
And live in perfect harmony.

Why is it so difficult then
For men to learn something from them?

Word Pictures

His abode

Like the fragrance resides in the flower
Like the fire resides in the charcoal
So the divine resides in your heart
Then why search in forests?

Love is

Love is what the bee feels for the flower
Totally absorbed, he lets the petals close him in.
If love does not dissolve the ego
It is not love but selfishness.

Thou art

Thou art the ocean vast and deep
I am a tiny helpless fish
I understand nothing at all except
Outside of you I am instantly dead.

Prayer is

Prayer is what the entire universe is doing
The suns and stars are the lamps
The forests spread the incense
The air fans the omnipotent deity.

Truth is

Everything in this world is true
It is created by the creator who is true
Remove the veil of appearances
And see the truth in its brilliance.

Illusion is

Like a line in the water
Like a bubble of water
All that is visible and temporary
Is an illusion and false.

Wisdom is

Wisdom is not found in books
Wisdom lies in being aware
Wisdom lies in obliterating self
To let divine light shine through

Life is

Life is an opportunity
That even gods long for
It is a bridge that helps the soul
Cross over from bondage to freedom.

Body is

This body is the temple of the living god
Take care of it and keep it clean
Make sure that it is not polluted or misused
By undesirable elements.

Pain is

Pain is the treatment and the remedy
For the deluding disease of pleasure
Pain is the reminder of the purpose of life
Pleasure tends to lead you astray.